HOW TO MAKE YOUR FIRST ONE MILLION DOLLARS DROPSHIPPING

HOW TO MAKE MONEY ONLINE AND BUILD YOUR OWN $ 1MILLION - DROPSHIPPING ONLINE BUSINESS, E-COMMERCE WITH SHOPIFY FOR PASSIVE INCOME

FORD HOLDEN

Made with ♥ on the Notion Press Platform
www.notionpress.com

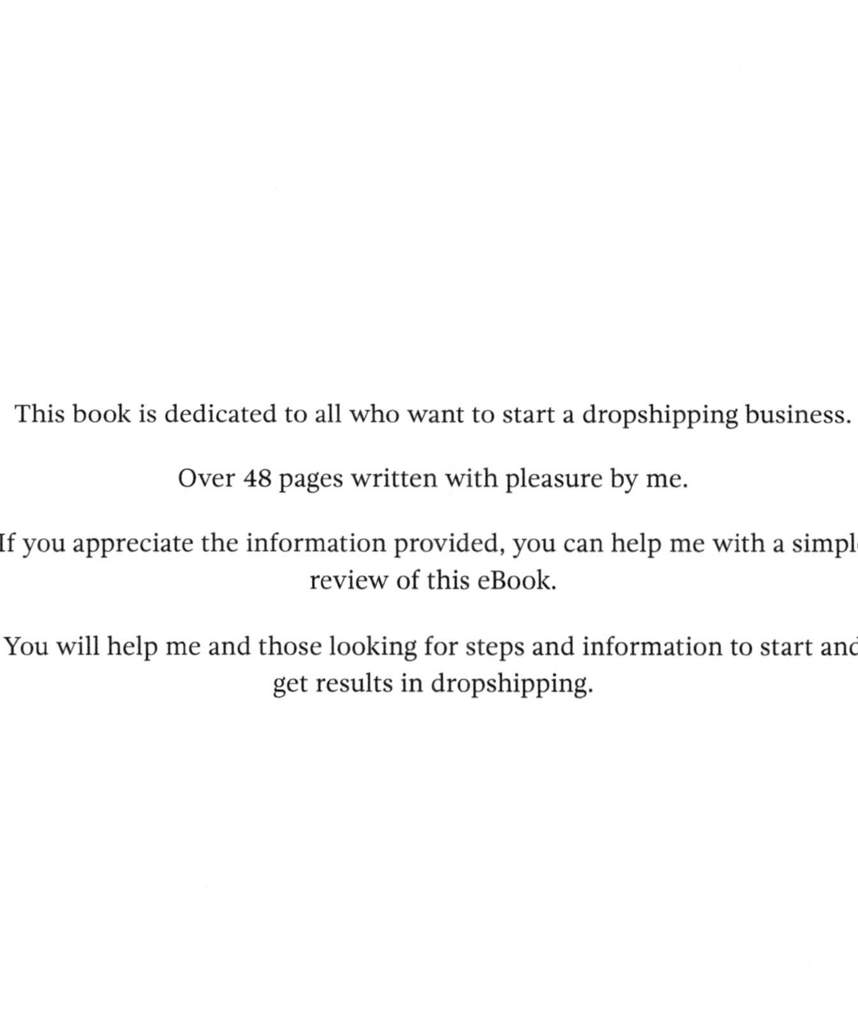

This book is dedicated to all who want to start a dropshipping business.

Over 48 pages written with pleasure by me.

If you appreciate the information provided, you can help me with a simple review of this eBook.

You will help me and those looking for steps and information to start and get results in dropshipping.

Contents

CHAPTER ONE

WHAT DOES DROPSHIPPING MEAN?

If you know nothing about dropshipping, this eBook is for you.

I think I have achieved quite good results in dropshipping. But I started entirely from scratch.

I managed to get over $ 1,000,000 in sales through my stores and students' stores.

With the help of over 6 years of experience in the field, I managed to offer to mentor. I supported a 1-to-1 mentoring program from almost 2018-2020. I even had countless consulting calls.

These 2 services are not valid at the launch of this eBook, but I will be back with them soon. Most likely after August 2021.

I say all this just so that you understand that you should trust the information I give you, and know that it is possible.

It is possible to get results from this level because I left too from 0.

After clarifying some of the essential things you need to know, we will move on to the steps you can follow to start dropshipping easily.

At first, I had no idea what dropshipping, marketing, advertising, Shopify, Facebook Ads, and many more mean. But I learned over time. Everything is step-by-step.

I wish I had access to information like that in the beginning, like this eBook.

This is one of the main reasons I am passionate about helping you.

So what exactly does the dropshipping business model mean?

Dropshipping is simply a business, like any other.

A complex business, however, is not for everyone. With the help of this eBook, you will not only find out if dropshipping is for you, but you will also be able to start this business if you decide that it is the right choice for you.

I want you to understand by now that dropshipping is not easy at all.

You may have heard this before, but it is more important than you think to understand that this business model is quite tricky.

I'm not telling you this to discourage you, but to make you ambitious. On average, less than 5% of those who try dropshipping manage to achieve sustainable results.

So, although it is nice to get excited when you see the results of others, think that it takes a lot of work and a lot of time to achieve great results.

As I said, I'll explain this to make you ambitious. Wouldn't you like to be part of that 5%?

No matter how hard it is, I would rather participate in the better team than stay in the mediocre crowd.

Also, at least when it comes to dropshipping, you will not succeed with the first store as a beginner in 99% of cases.

You have to assume from the beginning that it will be difficult. From the beginning, this business model requires a lot of knowledge in several areas, not just one.

That's why the beginning will be quite difficult. And because of that, you will need to work hard to get started. You need to build experience and learn each field. Each area helps complete the dropshipping business model.

I mean what else was mentioned early, Facebook Ads, marketing, advertising, etc? And that's why an online course can help you a lot and can greatly shorten your time and effort. As long as it is a well-chosen one.

HOW EXACTLY DOES THE DROPSHIPPING BUSINESS WORK?

Dropshipping is also known as the online sales business, which you can start with a relatively small budget. I say relatively small budget because you do not have to invest money in a stock of products.

This is the whole dropshipping scheme. You can sell online but without a stock of products.

How? Simple.

When you make a sale on your store, you will send the order data to a supplier who has the product you are selling in stock.

That provider will then take care of everything. He will send the product to your customer, directly from his warehouse. So you're kind of an intermediary—no more.

That's the majority of business it works. You buy cheaper, you sell more expensive.

This is where the profit comes from.

You find a product that seems to have potential and that you believe in, and you start promoting it, hoping that you will make sales.

If the vendor you find has that product and sells it for $ 13 for example, you could sell it in your store for $ 30. From here you make a profit of $ 17.

No net profit though, because you will have other costs besides the product.

But basically and simply speaking, this is drop shipping. Even though it is mentioned that it is a complex business. I will try to take things in stride for you. In everybody's language.

Most of you are new to entrepreneurship and business. I thought it might help to briefly discuss the pros and cons of dropshipping compared to other business models.

We start the next page with the disadvantages of dropshipping.

DISADVANTAGES IN DROPSHIPPING

1) **Your control over your business is reduced** - That's because you don't own the products you sell.

This disadvantage is not a critical one, but compared to stores that have stock, you do not have so much control available. You receive a total price from the supplier chosen for the product you are selling.

Let's say you want to sell a simple t-shirt. Your supplier gives you a total price of $ 8 per t-shirt and you decide that you could sell it for $ 25 with a $ 17 profit margin.

The idea is that many things are part of the process of creating a simple t-shirt. From the material used to the employees used, the warehouse, equipment, and so on. All these things that make up the whole process can be optimized typically.

However, in the case of dropshipping, you do not have so much control over that shirt.

You can only negotiate a small price with your supplier, while a store that produces the product alone, could optimize every part of the whole process.

2) **Customer service is complicated** - Since the delivery time is not so good, customers will give you big headaches in most cases.

You will have many emails you need to respond to and many problems you need to clarify if you do not focus on your delivery time properly.

However, this disadvantage can be solved, especially over time. As long as you have a delivery time of fewer than 2 weeks, it is acceptable for a start.

It is ideal for reducing the delivery time to a maximum of 10 days. However, this may depend on several factors. Where do you send the product from and to which countries do you send it?

I do dropship from China to America.

So I take products from China and sell them in America.

It is possible to detail this decision later, but at the moment you should know that your goal is to reduce the delivery time to less than 2 weeks.

However, I recommend that you do not join the group of those who are stressed because the delivery time is long, but they have not even started selling anything yet.

3) **Profit is usually low** - A good profit in dropshipping is about 20%. If you see a 30-40% profit, I assure you it is a particular case.

Not that the 20% profit would be a bad one, but some want to brag. Profit is not necessarily low, but limited, rather. That's because you don't have that much control, mainly.

You can't control costs product, delivery costs, or delivery time as much as you would like.

However, if you are happy with a profit of $ 20,000 on sales of $ 100,000, we can move on.

THE ADVANTAGES OF DROPSHIPPING

1) **Simple and quick to get started** - Even though it is a slightly more complicated model even than a regular online store with stock, it is simpler and faster to get started.

That's because it doesn't require much hassle to get started, compared to an online store with stock.

At a regular store with stock, it takes quite a while to contact many suppliers to decide the best choice, given that you want to buy stock.

To negotiate the price in blood, to compare offers and make decisions for the packaging of the product, to think about the order processing system, to decide and conclude a contract with a delivery company, plus others.

When it comes to dropshipping, it's a kind of plug-and-play. You choose the product and you can start the sales the very next day.

2) **You can start with a small budget** - Although many complain about the budget even in dropshipping, I assure you that a stock store owner would punch himself when he hears that you are afraid to start an online store for only $ 500. You can even start dropshipping with $ 500.

We will discuss the ideal budget in more detail shortly, but to give you a little idea now, an Online store with a stock requires an investment of at least $ 2000- $ 3000.

This is in clear cases. Usually, the minimum budget is $ 5000 if you want optimal chances of success and you want to have a good start.

3) **It is a flexible business** - That's because you can pivot from one product to another in just a few days.

This a big advantage that you can't achieve with regular stock stores.

What do you do if you buy a stock of 2000 units for a product and you can't sell it anymore or something happens?

What do you do in dropshipping if you can no longer sell a product or something happens? Move on to the next one.

In conclusion.

I wanted to offer you 3 advantages and 3 disadvantages of dropshipping, so that you can better understand how things are, especially when compared to an online store that has stock.

However, you don't have to complicate things. As in any other situation, there are advantages and disadvantages. In dropshipping, things have a pretty good balance.

What you can do is improve your knowledge with the help of the information provided. Don't try to complicate things.

If you have read everything carefully so far, I want to congratulate you for a second!

It is important to mention that your interest and the seriousness with which you treat the situation, will have a great impact on your results.

I will continue to clarify some of the essentials, and then we'll move on to the exact steps you can take to get started. Dropshipping.

DELIVERY TIME IN DROPSHIPPING

Going back a little to more details about the time and methods of delivery in dropshipping, I want to clarify a few more things.

As I said earlier, many create big problems because of the long delivery time, when they haven't even started selling, or at least learning how to set up a correct store.

Don't get me wrong, it's important to know the dangers and obstacles of a business before you start, but some make it a reason to give up.

I hope you're not one of them. And yes, your order delivery and processing time will not be so good, to begin with. But it's normal.

To clarify, the **processing time is the interval from the time the order was placed until it was delivered to the courier for delivery. Delivery time is strictly the interval in which the courier delivers the order after you have delivered it.**

Being in dropshipping, the only step in the order processing part that you can influence control is the interval in which you place the order on Aliexpress or to your supplier. This step is the only one that is part of the order processing time and that you can control.

The rest is taken care of by your supplier, and this is one of the reasons why you need the best supplier

However, it is perfectly normal for the processing time and delivery time of your orders to improve both with your store, and especially with your experience in dropshipping.

Let's take them a little bit now, we're talking about time processing. As I said, the only processing time that you control is the interval between the moment the order is placed in the store by the customer and the moment you forward the order to Aliexpress or the supplier you have.

You may be wondering now how to send orders from your store to Aliexpress. Do you place them manually?

You work with an application "DSers" that will do this for you almost automatically.

Now that you understand how to process orders received from customers, I have one more thing to mention about processing.

It is important to always allow 12 hours before sending orders received to Aliexpress. Specifically, when a customer places an order in your store, you want to wait 12 hours before entering the application and sending orders on Aliexpress.

Why?

Because...

You want to make sure you give your customers time to change their minds or find out if they did something wrong with the order or the completed address.

That's why you always want to check the emails and messages received from customers, every time before placing orders on Aliexpress.

In conclusion, it is important that every time you have to process the received orders, you should proceed as follows:

1. Check the email address of your store to make sure there are no emails received and unresolved from customers
2. Check your Facebook page and make sure there are no messages received and unclarified from customers;
3. Enter the DSers application to process orders on Aliexpress and only sends orders that are more than 12 hours after they have been placed.

We now move on to delivery time.

As I said, the delivery time is strictly the interval in which the courier delivers the order after you have provided it.

After your supplier handed it to them, in our case. What interests you here is to work with Aliexpress for a start.

I still believe that Aliexpress is the most affordable method for beginners who want to validate products.

The perspective you should have is this:

You will validate the product with Aliexpress, and then you will contact a private agent after you see that your product works.

That is, you will test the product to see if it is a good product or not. Whether or not it brings sales. Whether or not it's worth continuing with. That means validating a product.

Throughout this validation process, you will only work with Aliexpress, you will use Aliexpress and the method I presented in the video attached above to send the received orders.

Then, after validating that the product is a good one and worth continuing with, your goal is to reach a minimum of 10 orders per day.

As soon as you approach 10 orders per day, you want to contact a private agent. A private agent is also a supplier but usually does not work on Aliexpress. A private agent is usually more suitable for the simple fact that he has worked in dropshipping and knows what it's about.

You can find agents like this through Facebook groups. Join Facebook groups about dropshipping and post there that you need a private agent + mention your current volume of 10 orders per day.

You will then contact several such agents. The idea is to talk to more people and choose the most advantageous offer for you and your product. Give them the necessary details and find out the price of each one.

Then find out what their system is, how it works, what their delivery time is, how the delivery method sends the products, and how they proceed with returns. Then compare all the information received from all the agencies you spoke to and you will then be able to choose the best one.

However, until you reach 10 orders a day, you will need to process everything through Aliexpress.

The delivery method I recommend is ePacket. I do not recommend that you send products with a delivery method other than this.

You will see on Aliexpress what delivery methods are available for each supplier.

Because when you search for a product on Aliexpress, you will notice that several different suppliers sell that product. You want to choose the best supplier from those available.

The provider that has the best rating, the best reviews, the best price, and the ePacket delivery method.

If your supplier is good, they should deliver all your orders to the US in about 2 weeks via ePacket.

With a private agent, you can deliver even in 10 days. When you go to a private agent, you want to be interested in the YunExpress delivery method.

YunExpress is another delivery company, better and more efficient than ePacket, but also a little more expensive.

I think we've talked a lot about delivery and processing time in dropshipping.

However, we need to clarify a few more things about the budget, the right mindset, and a few more things before moving on to the exact steps to get started. dropshipping.

We start with the next page to discuss the ideal budget for a beginner.

THE IDEAL BUDGET FOR DROPSHIPPING

Okay, I've come to the budget. Possibly one of the most common questions is "**what is a good budget to start with?**".

I will simplify things as much as possible. You can start dropshipping for as little as $500. This is the minimum I can recommend, not the ideal.

This minimum can give you a few chances but you will quickly run out of money if you can't feed your budget every month.

A good budget starts at $ 1000 and up. The ideal budget I recommend is $ 1500. This ideal budget of $ 1500 gives you **optimal chances of success.**

With a budget of $ 1500, you have greater certainty that you will have enough for the creation of the store, the creation of advertising, advertising, and even your personal development.

From $ 1000 I can recommend you buy the course to invest in your personal development at the beginning, and then to have an ok budget for the other things as well.

However, if you want to take a risk and you can't wait, you can make this move from $ 700.

A budget is significant for any business you want to start. You need to know precisely how you will use that budget and try to estimate your expenses.

For drop shipping, I said to help you with the chart below.

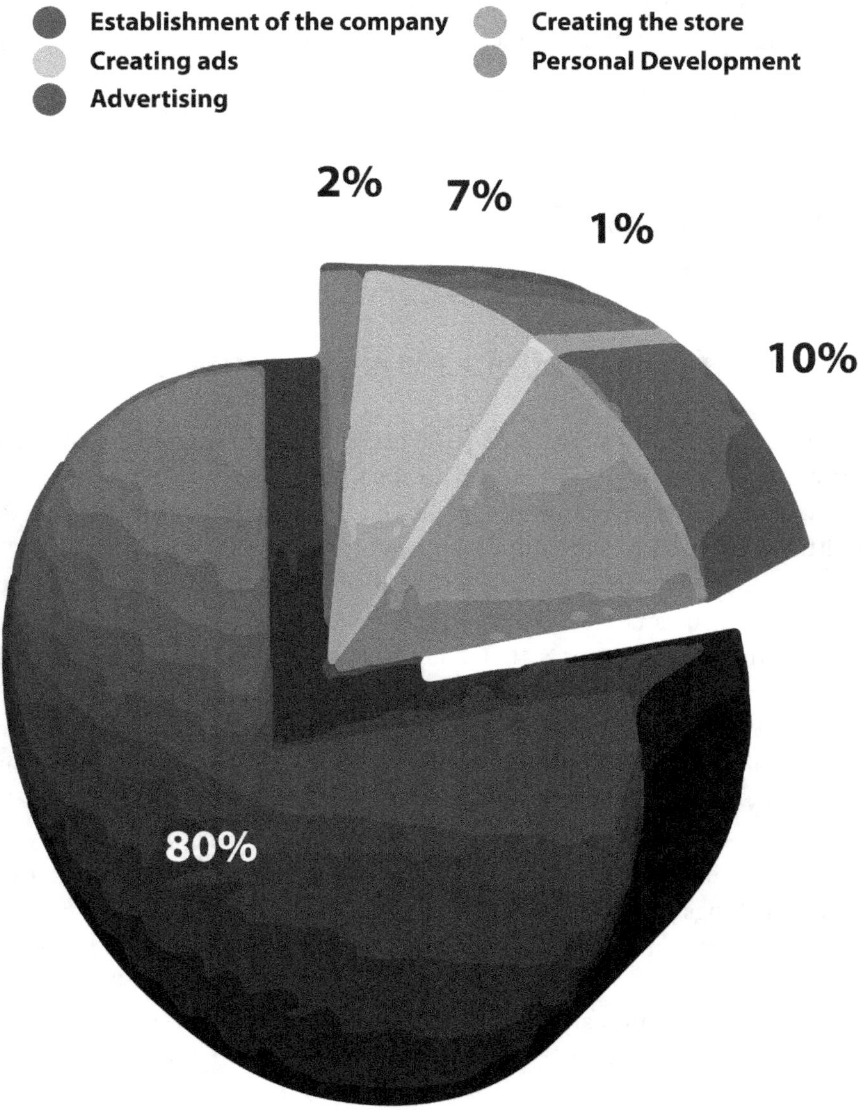

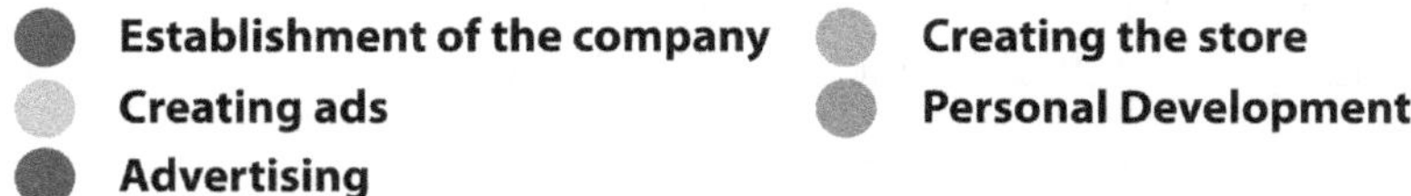

The graphics are, however, only an estimate. Just to give you an idea of how you should split your budget.

This seems to be the most effective strategy to optimize your budget in dropshipping, as a beginner.

As you can see, we have included 10% for personal development. **Your education is, in fact, in the first place.**

You will not invest most of your initial budget in your development and education, but it is the most important part of the whole process.

In vain you have a budget of $ 5,000 and you think you are equipped in all respects if you do not have as your main goal your education and personal development.

But do you know what investment is more efficient in your personal development than that of time and effort?

Investing money.

As long as you carefully choose the material in which you want to invest part of your budget, you can't go wrong.

I had the first great results in dropshipping, just after investing in a paid course.

One of the reasons for this phenomenon is that we humans simply capitalize on more paid information than free information.

If I offer you something for free, in most cases, you will not offer so much interest and so much seriousness.

But if you know you paid a sum of money, whatever it is, for a material that should get you to develop personally, treat the whole situation completely differently.

Now that we've clarified everything you need about the budget, let's clarify a few things regarding the company, even if you are not yet 18.

CHAPTER TWO

ESTABLISHMENT OF THE COMPANY

Many of you ask me if I can start even if I'm not 18, or what to do with the company if I'm not 18. I will not discuss this much because the idea is very simple.

I also started in this field at the age of 17. Think that it will take you a long time anyway until you start producing some results. It is ideal to set up your company from the very beginning, and for this, someone from your family or someone close to you can help you if you are not yet 18 years old. Someone major can set up the company in his name, and you can operate everything. At 18, he can transfer the company to your name. Simple.

However, two as I said, it will take some time until you reach tangible results. Especially if you're under 18. So I don't know if I'd bother too much with the company in your case. At least not before I realized I had potential and at least achieved the first results.

What I can tell you is that you would not be the first or the last to want to achieve some results before setting up the company.

And it doesn't seem abnormal to me. However, I can't recommend this to you. It is ideal to set up your company from the beginning.

So? How do you set up your company?

Simpler than you think. Many are very scared of this side. There is nothing strange, nothing impossible, and nothing risky.

Try to imagine this company as your high school student card. In that notebook, you had all your averages, all your results as well as information about yourself and your profile. Same with the company.

You need a company to record all your results, your income, your business, and other such information. So simple.

The only difference between the two is that you didn't have to pay tax on your student card. Or were you? Haha.

Now it is even easier to set up a company because it is no longer mandatory to deposit the share capital. I won't go into details about that, since it doesn't matter anymore.

There are practically 2 methods to set up your company, the method you choose depends on your budget.

The first method would be to do a Google search.

Do a Google search and see the exact steps to start a business.

The second method is to hire someone who is an expert in the field to set up the company for you.

I used the second method for both companies.

As I said, it depends on your budget and the plans you have. You can move faster if you hire someone, and you have that certainty that everything is fine.

You can't even say you want to do it because you'll learn something. You will not open companies every month so you need to know what the process is. And if you get to open the second one, you can most likely hire someone to take care of it for you. But like I said, it depends on your budget.

I would say you can go for the second method if you have a budget of almost $ 1500.

ACCOUNTANCY

I didn't think I'd include anything about accounting in this eBook, but I'll touch on a few things quickly.

As with the establishment of the company, accounting is nothing to be afraid of. You will need an accountant, but it will not cost you a fortune. And no, you can't do your accounting.

The cost of the accountant will increase at the same time as your sales volume, so don't be scared of that either.

The important idea, however, is that the accountant you choose is an extremely important pawn in your business.

Here it is not necessary to choose the cheapest option. You don't want to have problems or hassles in the future. There is no need to choose the most expensive option.

Choose the right one.

Starting with the next page, I will start discussing the branches that make up this business model.

CHAPTER THREE

THE BRANCHES THAT FORM DROPSHIPPING

It was mentioned at the beginning of this eBook that dropshipping is a complex business and that you need knowledge in many areas.

I want to discuss a little more about the branches that make up this business model - dropshipping.

What knowledge should you have to be successful in dropshipping?

By branches, I mean anything that requires knowledge and experience to achieve results in dropshipping.

To be successful in dropshipping, you need experience in:
- Shopify
- Facebook Ads
- Advertising
- Marketing
- Branding
- Copywriting
- Communication
- Social media

I will detail each branch right now. I hope you never thought that Facebook Ads and advertising are the same things. I will clarify things for you.

1. Shopify

Shopify is simply a platform with which you will open your online store. On Shopify you will have your store, through Shopify your orders will enter and there you will see all the results and statistics of your store.

There is no great engineering here, you will learn the platform over time. It's not as vital as advertising, for example, but we still had to talk about it briefly.

2) Facebook Ads

Facebook Ads is simply the platform on which you will run ads, through which you will advertise your products, your store. Many confuse things, it is not so important to know Facebook Ads.

It is more important to know advertising and marketing.

Facebook Ads is just the platform through which you will run most of the advertising, especially for beginners. Nothing more than that.

It is important to know the platform, its options, its policies, how to use it, and so on.

But those who have good results, I assure you that they are not good at Facebook Ads. They are good, in fact, in advertising and marketing.

If you have good knowledge of advertising and marketing you will be able to have good results in almost any advertising platform.

Facebook Ads is based on just one advertising platform, like any other.

3) Advertising

One of the most important branches. Your advertising skills are extremely important when it comes to the success of your business, especially in dropshipping.

Usually, advertising goes hand in hand with marketing. That's because you can't use one without the other, but it's important to know the differences between the two.

Advertising strictly depends on your ability to promote your business, store, or product through various methods, paid or free.

It matters a lot to develop your ability to promote your services, products, or store.

However, my opinion is that the best way to develop your advertising skills is through practice. That's because everything can depend a lot on a case-by-case basis.

From product to product, from store to store. If you are trying to learn from YouTube how to promote on Facebook, there are only a few things that can help you.

What will help you the most from the videos on YouTube will be the information on how to use Facebook Ads, plus other details about the platform.

I'm not saying that strategies won't help you, but most of the time your situation will be different.

I'm not saying that strategies won't help you, but most of the time your situation will be different. That's because it all depends on the situation, as I said.

So I suggest you focus more on practice and experience when it comes to advertising.

Don't try to keep running after all sorts of strategies. Strategies are good to try, but experience from practice is much better and effective in the long run.

So try to learn from everything you do. Out of every $ 10 invested. From every strategy tried. Always try to think strategically, to understand why you get the results you get, and to realize how you can improve.

The biggest mistake you can make in advertising is to work blindly. Not having a personal strategy, control, a clue about the things you do. The decisions they make. The strategies you apply and why you apply them.

In advertising, if you don't learn from every move you make, it's like throwing money out the window. Always try to find a purpose for all the things you do and always have a concrete reason behind every decision you make.

However, in advertising, you will never be successful without skills in...

4) Marketing

The most important element of the whole equation. That's because you can't have effective advertising without marketing skills.

Mentioned that it is important to know the difference between the 2, to know how to apply them.

You've already learned what advertising is all about.

Marketing, simply put, is the process by which you identify your ideal client and determine how you can solve their problems, satisfies needs, or how you can help them achieve a better life and a better version of it.

Does it sound complicated?

It's not that complicated. However, as with advertising, much of the experience will come from practice.

However, when it comes to marketing, here you can learn more things that will be useful if you watch videos on YouTube, read books, or use other materials.

Given that advertising and marketing come bundled, I thought of a way to say it so you can better understand them.

Advertising helps you reach your potential customer, and marketing helps you convince that customer to buy your product or service.

With all this in mind, you now understand why it is useless to use the best advertising method if you do not know how to convince your customers to buy. Advertising is just the way you choose to promote your products. **Marketing is magic.**

Marketing is about the image or video, the text, and the offer that should convince customers to buy.

The next element, almost as important as marketing, is branding.

5) Branding

As I said, an element almost as important as marketing. However, it is not used to its full potential in dropshipping in most cases.

That's because branding depends on the identity of your brand. The identity of your store. The way it is presented to your store, the feeling it gives you, and the emotion it inspires in you.

When we talk about branding, we are talking about feelings, emotions, colors, graphics, identity. That means branding at its core.

Just as iPhones mean superior quality, fabulous design, high status, everything is superlative.

Even if the price is superlative, you buy it because you want to receive the same feelings, you want to experience that premium emotion, you want to be part of the group of those with high status.

Branding is built over time, you have to be very patient when it comes to it. It's just like a child. Branding grows easily and with continued perseverance.

I was saying that it is not used to its full potential in dropshipping because in most cases, especially as a beginner, you will not build a real brand by dropshipping. You will change the winning products in a few months the difference.

However, it also helps in dropshipping to have branding knowledge. Your store will look different, it will be presented differently, it will give you a different look feeling.

You can learn more about branding from YouTube videos, books, and other materials. But as with the others, you will learn more over time through practice.

What I recommend, however, is to study big brands like Apple, McDonald's, Rolls-Royce, and others. Study the identity of each brand and try to realize the feelings it offers, the emotions it offers, what it wants to convey exactly. This is one of my favorite exercises.

6) Copywriting

Copywriting is the art of presentation in words. No matter what you want to present or explain in writing, it's all about copywriting.

Copywriting is about how you formulate sentences, how you choose your words, structure paragraphs, and more.

You even keep spelling and how easy it is to make people understand what you want to convey through the text. No matter what you want to convey in writing, your knowledge of copywriting will help you tremendously.

Referring to dropshipping, copywriting will help you a lot in creating descriptions for the products you want to sell. Copywriting plays a vital role in your persuasive power in writing. No skills and knowledge in copywriting, weak will be your chances of convincing someone to buy your product.

Good copywriting skills help a lot in more effective marketing. I love copywriting. I'm super passionate about it, I see it as an art.

Art of communication and persuasion in writing. Don't you think that these 2 things matter a lot? The way you communicate and your power of written conviction?

7) Communication

As mentioned earlier in copywriting, communication is a vital element not only in dropshipping but in anything else you want to achieve.

I will not go into too much detail about this branch because it is clear why it is important. You will need communication in places when it comes to dropshipping.

Talking to influencers on Instagram, sending an email, keeping in touch with your accountant, with your supplier, all require at least a small communication skill.

You can easily develop your ability to communicate through YouTube videos and the like.

8) Social Media

No wonder you need knowledge on social media as long as you want to be successful in dropshipping. By social media, I mean Facebook, Instagram, TikTok, YouTube, and others.

You need to learn what works on these platforms, what types of content work, videos, or pictures? You need to learn what kind of approach works on each platform. What video sizes are suitable for each platform. Concrete example - on Facebook, the interval to capture a user's attention is about 3-4 seconds, while on TikTok it is less than 2 seconds.

You don't have to complicate things, though. Everything may be chaos in your head now and everything may seem too much to understand. Is OK. You can take things to step by step.

You don't have to know everyone's platform in part from the very beginning. It is enough to focus on just one to achieve great results.

However, I hope that now you understand much better not only what exactly dropshipping is made of, but also what each branch requires and what you should consider developing your skills for each element.

The next and last thing we need to discuss before moving on to the exact steps is the mentality. We are talking about the mentality suitable for success in dropshipping, starting with the next page.

CHAPTER FOUR

THE RIGHT MINDSET FOR SUCCESS IN DROPSHIPPING

I want to start by not believing how much I have discussed the mentality in the course for beginners. Almost every module has a video included for mentality just about that topic. Plus a whole module included just about the necessary mentality for success in dropshipping. That's because it's all about mentality if we take it rationally.

Success consists of **2 parts of mentality** and only one work. The mentality you have is the clear reason that determines whether or not you reach results.

I don't want to give in to spiritism and crazy stuff, but you have to understand that your mentality is the most important, no matter the situation, not just in dropshipping.

The mentality is practically related to the perspective you have on things. I could write about mentality for hours without stopping.

There we also discussed in more detail the reason most fail in dropshipping. In short, it does not offer things the seriousness and involvement required

I'm trying to give you some more concrete mental tips.

Perseverance keeps your mindset and plays a key role in your results and success.

Let's say you are told to find a product that can completely change your life **only after testing 8 without success.**

What would it be like to stop at the 7th product tested, knowing that the 8th is the one that will change your life?

Because that's what dropshipping is all about.

If you come across a winning product that you can scale a lot with, that's all you need to get big results. Logically, you didn't stop at only 7 products tested.

That's what you should always assume, no matter what the situation. Always assume that the next step/strategy/store/product is the one who will emerge the winner.

What if it's not next? Assume again that it is the following. I never want you to stop at the 7th product when the 8th may be the one that could it changes lives forever.

Another aspect of the mentality is burning desire. By burning desire I mean that strong feeling which you sometimes have when you want something with all your heart. By burning desire I mean that strong feeling which you sometimes have when you want something with all your heart. For a successful mindset, you need to train to have that burning desire more often.

Have a burning desire to grow continuously, to work more on yourself and your business, a burning desire to achieve results. To wish with all your heart to wake up in the morning and start working on your dream and what you want to achieve.

To fall in love with the whole process to achieve success.

As it is, with many failed attempts, it is important to love the process. If you do not love the process, you will never be able to conquer it.

One last piece of advice I give you about mentality is to think long-term.

Just imagine how much all this knowledge will help you in the future. All the skills you will develop in marketing, advertising, branding, copywriting, and so on. **All this will help you immensely no matter what you do in the future.**

It is a successful mentality to see the full side of the glass and turn things around in your favor.

That's about the right mindset for success in dropshipping. You understand at least what exactly the mentality is, why it matters so much, what you should consider and how you can work on it from now on.

We are now moving to the long-awaited moment...

THE EXACT STEPS TO START DROPSHIPPING

Ok, what are the steps to get started in dropshipping now? What are the exact steps to choose a product with potential, open a store, and test that product to start sales?

I will discuss one by one each step that a stranger must follow to be able to set up a functional store with a product that has potential.

Going back to the exact steps now, you would think that the first step is to create an account on Shopify or something similar.

You must first choose the product you want to test.

Not mentioned so far in this eBook, but there are 3 great ways to have a store in dropshipping.

1) General Store

A store that tests every possible product. It does not have to be in a certain category.

2) Niche Store

A store that focuses on a particular niche. Test products only in the category of animal lovers (as an example).

3) One-Product Store

A store that focuses on just one product. That's the only product you sell.

I will not discuss the advantages and disadvantages of each method, but you will better understand things along the way.

The strategy we will use is a combination of methods 2 and 3.

We will start with a One-Product store, a store centered around a single product that we trust and that we want to test, to maximize all our chances of success.

Then, after validating that the product brings sales and is one winner, we turn everything into a Niche Store. That's because we want to increase the range of products and the income of the store.

For example, if the product you choose at the beginning to test is a simple blanket, you will start the store with this. You'll have a store around that bed. You will discuss the benefits of that bed.

The special materials from which it is created and why it is so special and enormously comfortable not only to the touch but also when you squat in it.

Then, after testing that blanket and noticing that the product catches the public interested in such products, you can validate the store to turn it into a Niche Store.

You want to start adding other models of beds now, pillows of the same type, the same style. Sleep mask, pajamas for her, pajamas for him, even earplugs.

You want to turn that store from one only for lovers of extra comfortable beds, into a special and perfect one for lovers of quality sleep and even for those interested in extremely comfortable and quality house clothes.

You want to turn that store from one only for lovers of extra comfortable beds, into a special and perfect one for lovers of quality sleep and even for those interested in extremely comfortable and quality house clothes.

Your main product will still be the blanket, but now you will have more sources of income. You will start to think more strategically in terms of marketing. Think of special offers through which you can offer a blanket and a pillow at a special price (as an example of a simple offer). Or you can offer 3 different models of the best-selling beds at a lower price.

You will want to start focusing as much as possible on the average value of the order. But we will get there too.

I'm sure we've talked a lot about the types of stores, the strategy we will follow, and the general perspective you need to consider with your store. Let's finally get to our first step.

STEP 1 THE PRODUCT

The most important step in the whole equation. If the product is not the right one, it doesn't matter how good your ads are, your advertising, or copywriting skills.

At least not in dropshipping. The product is responsible for all the results you see in dropshipping.

Everything starts from the product. You need to ensure your chances of success with the chosen product. You don't have to limit yourself to one category/niche. You need a well-developed criterion for selecting products.

Some beginners tend to ask about the niche of products to choose from. Whether to go on products for animal lovers or household products, as an example.

But, at least in dropshipping, the product is more important than the niche in every situation.

In vain are you in a prosperous niche if your product is not a good one? At the same time, there were products from extremely strange niches that would still achieve very great results.

Now that you understand how important the product is, the next step is...

STEP 2 SELECTION CRITERIA

Those are some exact features that a product must meet to choose it. This is the method by which you can maximize your chances of success. We need to talk about this before moving on to the actual search methods products.

With the best possible criteria, you can increase your chances of success. **With a poor criterion, you will reduce your chances of success.** So simple.

2.1. Problem Solver

This means that the product solves a real problem for a certain audience. This is the first criterion that I detail and recommend. It is a criterion that helps beginners in dropshipping a lot. You will better understand why immediately.

As I said, a problem solver means a product that solves **a real problem for a particular audience.**

As a concrete example, **a heated vest is a solver problem because it solves the problems of extremely low temperatures and the cold issues that people face every year.**

I will continue to discuss this product for the following criteria.

The idea of this criterion is to think logically and rationally. Don't forget that we will also move on to the product search method.

Imagine a person who might be interested in your product and think logically if the product would solve a real problem for that person.

The bigger the problem it solves, the greater the persuasive power and potential of the product.

2.2. Massive Market

The following feature from your criterion must be one to ensure the largest possible market for the product.

That is, your product must have a market as large as possible, and an audience as wide as possible.

You don't want to focus on very specific products, that have a small audience. The lower the product market, the higher the costs promotion will increase and it will be harder for you to sell that product anyway. Make sure you can sell that product to as large an audience as possible.

2.3. Sensitive / Passionate Niche

This feature depends on the category of product you choose. You will increase your chances of success if you focus on products that have a sensitive audience or are passionate about.

A sensitive audience means an audience that is facing a certain problem. Examples specifically, back pain, cold due to winter, etc.

If the audience is sensitive, it will be much easier for you to sell your product.

That's because those people are looking for a solution to the problem they have. The problem they may or may not be aware of. Even if you are not aware of a particular problem, when you see a product that addresses a sensitive niche, and you are part of that category, you will instantly realize that you need that product.

A passionate audience means an audience that loves a certain thing to the fullest. A super passionate audience for something. A concrete example is the niche of animal lovers is one of the most passionate audiences.

Another concrete example is the niche of hiking lovers. People can be extremely passionate about things like that. They can love the products that can maximize their experience during a hike.

When you are extremely passionate about a certain thing, you will be much more open and easy to convince in buying a product that has a connection with that thing.

2.4. Profit margin

Undoubtedly, profitability is ultimately the most important element. You want to include in the product selection criteria something related to the profit margin that the product must meet.

The profit margin you need is a minimum of $ 15. How do you calculate the profit margin?

You need to know first what the total cost of your product is. You have to go to Aliexpress and look for the product you are interested in, then choose a supplier that seems to be ok in terms of reviews and orders, and calculate the total cost of that product.

The cost of the variant + the cost of delivery to the US with ePacket + $ 1 margin of error = TOTAL PRODUCT COST

Now that you know the total cost of the product, it's easy to see what the profit margin is.

That's why you want to get an idea of your competitors. Look for other dropshipping stores that sell the same product and see what price they sell it for.

Make sure you add the product to your cart, checkout, and select a delivery option. Many stores have the product at $ 15 but still, ask for $ 7 for delivery. After finding out the total cost of the product and the average selling price of the product, see what the difference is.

If your product has a total cost of $ 10 and an average selling price of $ 19.99, means that the profit margin is only $ 10.

As I said, you're interested in a margin of more than $ 15. The perfect range you want to be in is $ 20- $ 25.

2.5. New product

Another feature that you want to add to your criteria because it can increase your chances of success, is that for new products.

The idea is simple, you don't want to focus on products older than 12 months.

Search YouTube for the product you consider and you will find videos. Look for more product name variants if that's not enough to give you an idea. Then see when the videos with the product you consider have been posted. You should not watch videos older than 12 months.

The newer the product, the better your chances of success.

2.6. Multiple drop shippers are scaling the product right now

A feature with a longer name, but by far one of the most important.

I left what is best for the end. This means that more drop shippers (multiple dropshipping stores) will scale with your product right now.

Pay attention to the word "scaling". It is not enough for several dropshipping stores to have your product. That doesn't mean they sell it if they have it in-store.

You want to use YouTube again, but also Facebook and Google Trends to find out if the product is sold at high volume by other dropshipping stores at the moment. You can see on YouTube if you find recent videos that seem to have many views compared to the number of subscribers of the channel.

That's the idea for YouTube: Recent video + many views + few subscribers to the channel.

Concrete example: **If I see a video posted 3 weeks ago, it has a little over 10,000 views, and channel subscribers are only 750.**

The idea is to find that suspicious thing. It doesn't seem at all realistic to have so many views in just 3 weeks with so few subscribers. This may mean that the product is viral, one that is working well at the moment and is being sold in bulk by other drop shippers.

The idea is that it is much easier for a beginner to focus on products that are already working at the moment than to try something innovative.

Now that you understand much better what a product selection criterion means, what you should be interested and how to figure out if a product can have the potential to test it, we can move on to...

STEP 3 SEARCH METHOD

Now you know what interests you about a product, but you want to know how you can find products that meet the entire criteria we discussed.

The main and most important idea that you need to understand before telling you about any method, is that the selection criteria we discussed are much more important than the search method.

Everything is in order and it is important to know how to make a difference.

There are no search methods **good or bad.** The criterion is the magic one here. The methods are only effective or less effective. Almost any method can work, some are just more effective than others.

That is why there are dozens of methods by which you can search for products in dropshipping, but the criterion is always the most important.

The first method I offer you to use Wish, Etsy, and Aliexpress.

On Wish, you want to go to the "Popular" section to see popular products. You are interested in looking at products with a minimum of 1,000-2,000 orders. If you see a product that you think has potential, search for Aliexpress and go through the criteria.

On Etsy, you will find personalized products from which you can be inspired. You just want to look through the valid categories. See if something catches your eye. You won't usually find the same products on Aliexpress, but you'll find something similar in most cases.

But you can even work with Etsy providers. If you see a product that inspires you, but you can't find it on Aliexpress, contact the supplier from Etsy and see if it would be open to collaboration. In this case, you can have an even bigger advantage because there is no competition for your product.

On Aliexpress you want to look through the valid categories and sort the products by "Orders". See which products stand out and you can then go through the criteria.

On any of the 3 mentioned platforms you can even search for products, not just look through the valid categories and sections.

For example: If you are looking for something for your home or interior decor because you think it might work well now or you are passionate about it, look for something similar to "**interior decor**" or "**home decor**" On any of the 3 platforms.

This is the first method, accessible and completely free for a beginner.

The 2nd method, equally accessible and also free, is to use Facebook.

With this method you want to search on Facebook for such terms "Get yours now" / "i need this" / "i want this" / "buy it now" / "order now" / "get yours here" / "50% off now" / "50% off today".

The idea with this method is that you search Facebook for certain keywords used by dropshippers in their ads.

This way you can find new and scalable products.

Another important thing, however, is to enable the option to sort published videos. "**this month** ".

As with the first method, when you see something that could potentially go directly to Aliexpress to look for the product and start validating the criteria. **This method is even more efficient** because it offers you at least one competitor that already sells the product you are interested in.

You can better understand how well that product works because you will see directly what are the interactions with the product ad. How many likes, comments, shares, since it was posted.

STEP 4 SEARCH FOR PRODUCTS

Now that you have a selection criterion and you know how to look for products so that you can find something that has potential, **it's time to get to work!**

Start searching for products and add them to a document or Google Sheet. A better and safer method than choosing the first product that you think has potential is to make a list of at least 10 products that all have potential, **then choose the best one.**

So you got it right, that's your goal.

You start searching and you use the 2 methods until you reach 10 products that meet your criteria and have potential. Then you want to choose the best product out of those 10. That shouldn't be complicated.

Compare the products and the criteria between them to decide which would be the best choice you can have with the first product you want to test. You will then be left with a list of 9 potential products that you can return to if the first one doesn't work...

An important tip though, you never want to throw a product in the trash for no apparent reason.

Let's say you test a product and see that it doesn't work, you don't want to move on to the next product tested until it's clear to you why it didn't work first. It's like running blind.

Analyze the first product tested and try to figure out the things you did wrong or the wrong decisions.

See you at the 10 added products!

STEP 5 CHOOSING THE PRODUCT

I've already clarified this part a bit, but this is the next step. As soon as you reach 10 products that meet your criteria, you want to choose one of them to test. The idea is to quickly choose that product, you do not want to waste 4 days on this step. **Don't complicate things.**

A bonus would be if you are passionate about a certain product. If it's from a niche you're passionate about. This is because your marketing and copywriting will be much more effective if you are passionate about that product or niche.

Another bonus would be if a certain product offers you **certain confidence or activates your instinct.**

However, don't try to rely too much on this at first, as you have no experience.

Your instinct will become stronger over time. You will reach the level where you can decide in just a few seconds whether the product could have potential or not.

Now that you have chosen the product you want to test and in which you have to trust me, the hard part is over. The stressful and tiring part is over.

Now it's just a matter of getting things done. Store creation, setting advertising account, ad creation, and more.

If you got this far, you deserve big **CONGRATULATIONS!**

This ensures that you have completed the most important step in the entire process. Don't take it wrong, that doesn't mean you won't still squeeze your brains.

But hey ... it's part of the game!

STEP 6 KNOW THE AUDIENCE

An elementary step, but still omitted by most of those who already have some experience. I'm not saying anything about beginners...

You have chosen a product that you trust a lot and that you will test, you just don't want to go straight to creating the store now.

Don't you want to study the perimeter a little? To study the market a little? To get an idea of the profile of people interested in your product?

It seems to be one of the essential steps to have more effective marketing, copywriting and advertising, and to have as many chances of success as possible. So, things are pretty clear.

Try to get to know your audience, learn things about people who are interested in your product. Try to study them.

How they dress, how they talk, what interests they have, what words they use, what expressions they use, even how they think. All these things will help you put yourself better in the shoes of your ideal client, to achieve the goals you want.

How you all learn these things?

Use Facebook, Instagram, Google, blogs, and other sites to search for information about your audience.

If you have a niche product for animal lovers, search on Facebook for terms like **"dog love"**/ **"dog videos"**. Search Instagram for hashtags like **"# ilovepets"** / **"#catsanddogs"** / **"#petsforever"**.

Search Google for blogs and articles about how you should treat your pet, what food would be appropriate for your dog or cat, what gifts you could give them, or the like.

Make the most of all these methods and platforms to study your audience. To learn much better the words that your audience uses, the phrases they use, the content they are attracted to, the videos or images they catch best.

Write down all these things because they will be very useful in creating the store and creating ads.

Now you seem to be much better equipped to set up your first store. With a well-thought-out and chosen product, and well-done themes about your audience, you seem to feel much more confident. That is how it must be!

STEP 7 THE STORE

We reached the slightly more interesting part, the creation of the store. There will be a lot of quick steps we have to go through, but let's clarify a few things beforehand. Creating the store is not the most important part of the whole process. As I taught you, the product is.

Your store must be as simple and high quality as possible.

If you focus as much as possible on these 2 criteria, believe me, you don't need more than that, to begin with.

These 2 elements are the basis of a successful store. These 2 elements are the basis of a successful store. The goal of your store is to help customers buy the product they want, **in the simplest and fastest way possible.**

No interruptions, no weird stuff, no dubious animations or buttons. Beginners tend to complicate things, no wonder why, but try to understand from now on that the success of a successful store, in 90% of cases, lies behind the simple, fast, and intuitive structure. When you hear about all sorts of optimization strategies store, try to think rationally before pursuing them. By strategies I mean, for example, the method of adding needles trust badges (trusted icons) on the product page, under the button.

We, humans, are used to watching the flock of sheep, not asking too many questions, and **not thinking rationally unless we are put on the wall.**

My advice is to chew (think rationally) any movement heard before implementing it. And here I mean life in general, not just business or drop shipping.

Returning to the example given, trust badges are not necessarily bad. They are bad when you do not know how to use them correctly and when you do not think rationally. Many use the same image, and the same icons in each store.

This is a mistake. That's because every store, every product, every niche, and audience needs a different approach.

For example, in the beauty niche, you not only want to have different colors, slightly softer, simpler colors, such as **to stay** or **to stay.**

But also, you want to focus on **another style of icons**, a little friendlier, and be sure to include a cruelty-free icon if you can.

Cruelty-free means that your cosmetics have not been tested on animals.

What it looks like is **an important thing for this niche.** What I want to explain in this whole thing is that every niche is different, every product is different, and the audiences are different. You caught this.

So you will need different things from store to store. Please do not use the same image for trust badges at each store, as I gave that example above.

Before you start working on your store, before choosing the name and all, that is, now, assume that you want the whole store to be as simple, qualitative, intuitive, and resonate as much as possible with your audience.

So you will want to start studying massive brands in your niche.

If you are in the beauty niche, study brands like Kylie Cosmetics, BOOM by Cindy Joseph, Ulta Beauty, ColourPop, and others. A short Google search will answer many questions in most cases.

Bonus: and very fast.

Follow all these steps and you will ensure a successful store. One you will trust and one you can't blame if you don't get results. You will take it out of the equation and you will be left with the product or marketing (advertisements) to choose the problem because of which you have no results.

Because this is ultimately the formula for success, not only in dropshipping but online in general.

PRODUCT + OFFER + STORE = SUCCESS

The product matters the most. **If you have a good product, then you need to focus as much as possible on the offer and the marketing.**

The store is the last. His goal is simple, you can't fail as long as you follow some basic principles.

Now that you have a better understanding of the whole process of creating the store, let's go straight to the point.

STEP 8 STORE NAME

Again a simple but complicated step for many. We don't want to complicate things. I try to easily build a culture of shark entrepreneurs.

'Sharks' as I will call them.

Entrepreneurs are different and unstoppable.

Entrepreneurs who never have excuses, only actions at hand.

Entrepreneurs who never have excuses, only actions at hand.

Entrepreneurs who never have excuses, only actions at hand.

Because in the end, this is the necessary mentality. **You must be a shark.**

That's what it's about. These are the entrepreneurs I need next to me. However, we leave the motivational speech for the moment and return to the choice of name.

Maybe I'll launch some kind of ebook or dictionary of shark entrepreneurs. Maybe I'll launch some kind of ebook or dictionary of shark entrepreneurs.

Returning... The name you choose for your store will also be used as a domain.

If I want to have the name of the store **TheSHARK**, the will be **theshark.com.** So you need to make sure that the .com domain is valid when you want to decide on a certain name for your store. I recommend a .com domain because it has a higher trust.

A .com domain should not cost you more than $ 15 a year. I recommend you buy it from NameCheap. Search for NameCheap domain name search on Google. It is a page where you will be able to check if a domain is valid or not. You want to stay with that page open and immediately check every name idea that comes to mind.

Your criterion is simple.

Your name should be as simple as possible, easy to understand, easy to say, as short as possible, and as much as possible related to your audience or niche.

Get as much inspiration as possible from the brands in your niche and make sure that every name you check meets the mentioned criteria. Some examples of good names from massive brands would be **HiSmile from hismileteeth.com, GymShark from gymshark.com, AlyaSkin from aklyaskin.com.**

Notice how each of the mentioned brands meets the criteria mentioned above. Once you decide on a valid name, creates an email address of the store.

In my example, I would have something similar to **theshark@gmail.com,** or **contacttheshark@gmail.com,** or **thesharkbusiness@gmail.com.** You will use this email address to create all the necessary accounts for the store. NameCheap account, Shopify, etc.

Don't waste much time on this. Follow the criteria, get inspired by brands in your niche, and decide the name as soon as possible so that you can move on to more important things.

STEP 9 COLOR SCHEME

Your store must have a color scheme. That is one or two main colors on which the brand is based. **As Mcdonald's dominated yellow and red colors.** Nothing complicated here either.

Our method of inspiring us from massive brands will help you the most. See what main colors the brands in your niche use and be inspired by them. And the color scheme should resonate with your audience. As I offered the 2 colors as an example in the beauty niche when we talked about trust badges.

As a small bonus, you can use the free Google Chrome extension **"ColorPick"**. Search on Google. You can use the ColorPick extension to identify the color code of any color you like. If you see a certain shade of blue that you like, you can get the same color code to add to your color scheme.

Your scheme will consist of black and white, plus one main color and one secondary. **The main color** you want to use is for the most important things (eg the button to add the product to the cart). **The secondary color** you can use for other things or accents that are not so important. If you can't find 2 colors, you can limit yourself to one color main. And that's how it works perfectly.

The last thing, make sure you save your color codes somewhere in your scheme. It can be in a Google document, Word, or through a simple screenshot. Remember, don't complicate things!

STEP 10 STORE LOGO

This may be the step that gives the most headaches for most in the process of creating the store. **The point is, it's so easy to create a decent logo these days.** You don't need a lot of experience or design skills to create a decent logo.

Most are extremely confused because they try to start everything with the logo when they are not even sure of the name of the store and have not yet decided on a color scheme. As long as you follow the order of the process, everything should be fine.

We also have some criteria for a good logo in dropshipping.

Make sure your logo is minimalist, high quality, as unique as possible, and resonates with your audience. Sounds similar, doesn't it?

We are following the same process. The steps are similar when it comes to creating the store. By the most unique logo, I mean that you should try to have something special, something of his. **But it's not essential, just do it if you can and have inspiration.**

One important thing with the logo is that it should not be pulled by the hair. **It's not okay if you start to get frustrated and stressed when you create your logo.**

Keep your calm, confident and try to be as creative as possible while having a clear mind.

The first method that I offer you is to create your store logo. You can create a logo with Canva, totally free.

Quickly find a tutorial on YouTube on how to create a good logo in Canva. Don't be scared of this method, even if you have absolutely no experience and have never done it before, I still recommend you to try it. You may do better than you expected.

The second method, which I recommend you to follow only if the first one doesn't work or didn't turn out so well, is to create it automatically.

Some sites can make a logo for you in just a few seconds, automatically and for free. Search on Google "**Namecheap Free Logo Maker** " To try this method. The Namecheap option seems to be one of the most successful, but you can try others.

Search on Google "**Free Logo Generator**" And see what methods you can compare with the one offered by me.

The third method which I recommend, just in case you can't handle it at all or you don't want to waste time with it, it's to pay someone on Fiverr. Fiverr is a service platform. You can buy almost anything service, including one for creating logos. Search YouTube for a video on how to buy a Fiverr logo to get a better idea.

You have 3 good methods and effective to create a decent logo in less than 24 hours. Don't complicate the places!

Get to work quickly and efficiently. Some things matter much more than this step. Just make sure you follow the criteria provided.

STEP 11 SOCIAL PLATFORMS

Congratulations on your progress! If you have followed this eBook and completed all the steps so far, you deserve a big congratulations!

You now need to create the social pages, Instagram page, and Facebook page of your store. Nothing complicated here either, you are only interested in customizing them for a start.

And by customization I mean to add the logo and some essential details.

You don't have to start posting or banging your head more than that for a start. It won't help you at all. You can take care of this after you validate the product and see that it works.

For the Facebook page, you just need to add the logo to the profile and a cover photo. Nothing more to begin with. Make sure the profile logo is on a white background, 500x500. You can create this with Canva. If your logo has an icon, I recommend using only the profile icon.

Not the whole logo because it wouldn't be so well understood. If your logo has only text, use the full text.

For the Instagram page, add the logo again and a simple description of the page. Get inspired by brands in your niche and see what they use in the description of the Instagram page. Then add the link to your site.

STEP 12 BACKEND SETTINGS

It's time to create a Shopify account if you haven't already. We will now take care of the backend settings in Shopify. That is the settings behind your store.

Backend settings are divided into 2 categories:

1) Settings

2) Online Store

You can access both from your Shopify account. You can see them on the left side of the screen. I recommend you start with Settings. There you will have to go through each of the valid sections and make sure everything is set up properly.

In Settings, you will find the options General, Payments, Checkout, Shipping, and delivery, plus more.

Generally, you want to add some details about the store. Name, address, telephone number. All your company information, if you already have one. There you also want to change the currency (store currency) to USD.

The Payments you want to connect payment processors (Stripe and PayPal).

At the checkout, you can edit your checkout settings. How you want your store checkout to look like and what sections you want to include.

Shipping and delivery you want to set your shipping methods. The delivery methods that the customer can select at checkout. I recommend that you have a free delivery option for the best possible conversion. In progress, I offer 2 more delivery options to maximize the revenue and profit of any store.

The Taxes just make sure you don't collect taxes from any country. And that's about it. With the other options, you have nothing else to edit. You're done with settings, you can now go to the Online Store.

Online Store is divided into 6 sections: Themes, Blog Posts, Pages, Navigation, Domains, and Preferences. I will try to detail as much as possible here each section.

The Themes, you will want to select the theme of your store. In the next step, we discuss how you should customize the chosen theme. For now, you just have to choose one. Shopify themes are free or paid. Like free themes, I recommend Debut or Brooklyn. From the Themes section, you can go to Explore Free Themes and choose one of the 2 options mentioned. Anyone can work for any store. Like the paid theme, if you want to make such an investment, although it is not necessary, I recommend the Booster theme.

The Pages you will need to fine-tune the essential pages of each store. I mean Terms of Service, Privacy Policy, Refund Policy, Contact Page, and Track my order page.

Navigation you can edit the menus displayed on your store.

The Domains you will have to connect the domain purchased from Namecheap.

The Preferences add your store name, slogan, some product details, or the products you sell. And lastly, in the Facebook Pixel section, you will have to connect your Facebook pixel.

You're done with all the backend settings! It may have been a little longer here and with some hassle, but that's the first time.

STEP 13 THEME SETTINGS

I hope you have already decided on the theme you want to use. Among the free themes, I recommended Debut or Brooklyn. Like the paid theme, if you are a little more advanced and have the necessary budget, choose the theme Booster and you won't be sorry.

Now, the idea is simple when it comes to Shopify themes. That's because each theme is different, not only in appearance but also in settings.

Free themes like Debut or Brooklyn are not so different when it comes to settings.

However, if you choose the Booster theme, you will have much more control and many more settings there. That's because the Booster theme can replace the many applications you'll need in Shopify. We will also get to know the applications.

However, regardless of the theme you use, the theme settings are divided into 2 large sections.

The first section is the one you notice on the left when you go to customize the theme. The one that will always contain **Header** as the first editing option, and **Footer** as well as the last editing option.

This first section automatically changes depending on the page you are on. For example, on the product page, you will have different settings from those that appear on the main page of the store.

The second section from the theme settings is called Theme Settings. You can also find it on the left when you customize the theme. Given that the first section changes from one page to another, this 2nd section, **Theme Settings always stay the same.** That's because from there you will have access to the settings of the whole theme. That is, the global settings of the theme if you want to call it that. Options that you can edit, such as font and colors, and that change for the entire theme, not just on that page. These are the basic things you need to know to edit your chosen theme.

As mentioned, the settings and process can be a little or more different from one theme to another. However, you understand what the settings are and what you need to edit. So beat him! Imagine customizing your dream car. It's the same with the store. It will take you a few hours, but it will be fun and you will start moving faster and faster.

STEP 14 ADD THE PRODUCT

It's time to add the product to your Shopify store. Things should already look much better and everything should start to take on color.

I will divide this step into 4 smaller and easy-to-follow steps.

The first step is to choose the best supplier on Aliexpress for your product. Enter Aliexpress, search for the product, and open as many suppliers as you notice to sell your product. Then compare them with each other and stay with the best in terms of reviews, orders, and price.

However, make sure it delivers with **ePacket** by **DOOR**. Now that you have chosen the right supplier for your product, you want to add it to the store. Practically connect it to the store. For this, we will use an application, **DSers. DSers is an official Aliexpress application that works with Shopify.**

It connects your store and your product with the supplier you choose on Aliexpress. Like when you receive an order in the store, you can place it almost automatically directly on Aliexpress. The first complete step. We move to 2.

Step 2 you do a little research. Research means searching. For the second step, you want to search for as much content as possible with your product. Use YouTube, Facebook, Instagram, and Google to get as much content as possible. By content, I mean videos, images, and gifs with your product. The content you want to give you organize nicely on the computer, so you can then use it easily. You will need to use this content when editing product creation, ad creation, and even store editing. Both for 2. We move to 3.

Step 3 it's about creating the product description. You may have already thought that your product needs a description. You have to convince people who have chosen to enter your store, to buy your product. This is what the product description will do. It is a slightly more complex process than it seems. But try not to complicate things. The idea is that it will not work with a description taken from Aliexpress, or one copied in its entirety from competitors.

I recommend you create it yourself. If you can't speak English, you can use Google Translate. It would be good for you to be inspired by competitors who sell your product. But keep in mind that most people don't do that well.

A small bonus, I recommend the free extension for Google Chrome **"Grammarly"**. Search Google and use it. It will automatically ensure that you write correctly in English.

Another thing that I recommend and that is very important, **is to have paragraphs as short as possible.** Try to have paragraphs that are as short and direct as possible. Between 2-3 paragraphs should defend **a picture** or a **gif** with your product. You should not have more than 2 gifs in the product description.

It is important to compress all the pictures you use, not only for the product description but also for the entire store. Search on Google **"Free Image Compressor"** And you will find many options for this. Photo compression is important to have the best loading speed of your store. You don't want to make customers wait.

The 4th and last step to add the product is to do a final review of your product. Go to the product page in the store, the page that customers can access, and make sure everything is fine. The images section should be ok, the description should be fine and error-free, the images/gifs in the description to be ok too. I recommend you to do a review like this for absolutely any important step you take, not just for adding product, and not just in dropshipping. **A short review of only 1 minute can quickly get rid of big mistakes.**

STEP 15 SHOPIFY APPS

Shopify apps are like extensions of your store. They are actually like the applications you download on your phone. Your Shopify store can do certain things, but you can increase its limits with certain applications. Same with the phone. The phone's note-taking app is pretty good, but you can have something on an even higher level with an app. downloaded from the App Store or Play Store. Just like on the phone, Shopify apps are free or paid. Some you pay directly through Shopify, others will ask for your card details because they are paid separately.

To install apps, log in to your Shopify account, then go to Apps -> Shopify App Store. What you need to know about these applications is that you should not install too many. Try to limit yourself to what is strictly necessary. Too many applications will make your store difficult. You may even have problems with the store if you install inappropriate applications.

Remember that you can always use Google, YouTube, and any of the other resources we have provided during this eBook. For each application, you should be able to find some kind of tutorial or help material on YouTube or Google.

15.1. Easy GDPR + Cookie Bar

It is an application only for those who want or think they will expand in Europe with sales. If you only sell in the USA, it is not essential to install this application, although it is completely free and very easy to set up. You can find it on the Shopify App Store.

15.2. HideOut - Hide PayPal Button

An application only for those who use PayPal. It helps you better optimize your store by getting rid of PayPal shopping cart and checkout buttons that can confuse the shopping process. You can find it on the Shopify App Store. It only costs $ 1 a month.

15.3. InstantBuy

An application that adds a useful option to your store, totally free. Specifically, add another button to add the product to the cart, a button that will always be posted at the bottom of the screen, both on the desktop and the phone. You may have seen such an option in many other stores. It is an option found in the Booster theme, so if you chose the Booster theme you do not need this application because you will already have the option in the theme settings. Otherwise, you can find it on the Shopify App Store, it is a free application. You don't need to choose the paid plan.

15.4. Accountify

An extremely useful and incredibly affordable application. It helps you calculate the net profit of your store. It automatically connects to Facebook Ads and you can set the costs of each product you sell so that its application automatically calculates your daily, weekly and monthly profit. A completely free application, to my surprise. You can find it on the Shopify App Store.

15.5. Loox

The application you need to show reviews on your store. It's an application that costs $ 10 a month and you can use it to automatically import from Aliexpress or manual reviews for each product you have.

I recommend you to take the reviews on Amazon, write them manually on the store, and add a minimum of 20 reviews for your product. Not all should be 5 stars. The total rating of the product should be 4.5 stars.

15.6. Best currency converter

An application that you need for the price of your products to be changed automatically depending on the user's country. If someone from Romania enters your store, they will see the prices in LEI. Someone in Canada will see the prices in CAD. The app can increase the conversion rate of your store and is somewhere around $ 10 a month. You can find it on the Shopify App Store.

15.7. SweetUpsell

An application that helps you increase sales and profitability. The app costs $ 20 per month but will only take your money after the first sale generated by the app. So you can install it without any problems. It doesn't take your money until it makes you money

15.8. SMSBump

The application you need on any of your stores. Undoubtedly the best application I always use. **It is essential.** I don't go into details, but the app helps you send messages (SMS) to customers who drop out at checkout. An essential marketing step and SMS messages are tens of times more effective than emails.

15.9. Abandonment Protector

The last application I recommend is for email marketing. An application that helps you send emails. Especially customers who drop out at checkout. It's only $ 8 a month and you can find it on the Shopify App Store. and I recommend you to configure all 3 emails for abandonment at checkout. Now not only do you know exactly what the whole Shopify app is all about, but you also know the exact apps you need on your store.

We continue the next page with step 16 for creating ads.

STEP 16 CREATE ADS

I'm completely done with the store. Congratulations again on all the progress! You are doing an excellent job because you have come this far. This is the last step before promoting the store. You have chosen the product, you have set up your store, and now it is ready for promotion. Close...

You need ads with which to promote the product. I will give you 2 methods that you can use to create your ads.

The first method is a completely free one. You can use the content you got with your product from step 14. With those videos and pictures, you will make the ads you need on your own.

The most accessible video editing application, especially for beginners, is InShot on the phone. You can't find it on your computer. It is a free application. It may cost only 2$ to get rid of their logo on the videos you create. Although on Android I think you can get away with it if you see an ad of theirs, so it's free. **You can find many tutorials for InShot on YouTube.**

For those a little more experienced in video editing, you can use Adobe Premiere Pro It would be ideal, but not necessary. You can move even faster with InShot in some cases.

For image editing, you already know. Use for free **Canva** or Photoshop if you can and you know how to use it.

This would be the first method of creating ads. Create them yourself, completely free.

Regarding the actual ads you should create, I think you've already caught the idea. You need to be inspired by competitors and massive brands in your niche. **Each product is completely different.** For some products, images may work better than videos In most cases, however, videos work much better than images. So, take inspiration from competitors, see what worked for them and try to model what went well, but even improve things as much as possible.

The second method I offer you for creating ads, you guessed it, is a paid one.

In case you can't handle it at all or you want to move much faster, I offer you the service that I also use for commercials. my products.

They can help you with videos, images, gifs, even texts for your Facebook ads.

Waving Pandas. You can create an account, and then see all the details and prices of each service. As I said, you can handle the first method. But, if you want something qualitative and if you want to be sure that you can rely on advertisements, I would recommend you to choose the second method. This way you can make sure that you eliminate all the parts and that you can only focus on the product. If you follow my advice, your store should be a good one. If you choose the 2nd method for creating ads, you ensure good ads for your product. So, the only thing that can fail is the product. This way you eliminate all the variations from the equation and stay only with the product.

I assure you that you will be served with a high-quality service. You just already know that I only associate with that.

STEP 17 PROMOTION

You have reached the end! **I can already call you a shark of entrepreneurship**, but this step is at least as important as the others so far. In fact, without this step, you have worked in vain so far. You chose the product, you set up the store, you got ads, it's time for promotion, to get results. The most affordable methods for a beginner in dropshipping are Facebook Ads and Instagram Influencers.

The first method means promoting your product and store on Facebook. Through the Facebook Ads advertising platform.

The second method requires working with influencers to promote your product and store. Both methods can be used to test a product to decide if it works or not.

But the big difference between the two is your budget. It depends on your budget.

If you don't have a minimum budget **of $ 1.500**, I do not recommend starting with Facebook Ads as a beginner. Being an extremely complex platform, you will need a bigger budget to be able to start learning and get results.

If you have a budget of between **$1.000** and **$1.500**, you can still try Facebook ads, but your chances of success will not be so great.

Instead, with a budget below **$1.000**, I recommend you start with the influencers on Instagram.

Influencers are of 3 types:

1) Thematic pages

2) Micro-influencers

3) Macro-influencers

Document yourself better about each one and start working with them to test and validate the product, if you have a budget of less than **$1.000-$1.500**. Regardless of the method, you choose to use, I will try to give you some more general advice regarding promotion. The perspective you should have on promoting your product is one in **3 stages.**

The first is testing ads. Initially, you want to test different advertisements of the product while you realize whether or not the product brings sales. By doing this, you will not only realize the product itself, but also the advertisements used. I recommend using 3-4 different ads for your product, so you can study later results and improve things. Whether you choose to go for Facebook Ads or Instagram Influencers, these internships and principles can be applied to both.

Stage 2 is to study the results obtained. Results in which you have invested something from your advertising budget. In stage 2 you should already decide whether or not you can continue with the product. See if it brings sales and if it has potential.

It is perfectly normal not to be profitable in the beginning. You deal with profitability during internship 2, where you want to study the results obtained and start improving things.

You deal with profitability during internship 2, where you want to study the results obtained and start improving things. Let's take them one at a time.

AOV site depends on the improvement of the store and means Average Order Value. As an example, if you sell a $30 product, your AOV will be somewhere around $30.

Instead, if you sell a $30 product and offer another $5 complimentary product in addition to the main one, your AOV will increase to $35.

You want to focus as much as possible on this AOV (average order value), by adding more products that you can sell together with the main one. This AOV can make a big difference in the profitability of your store. With a single such optimization, you can go from unprofitable to 10-20% profitability.

The second thing, product ads. You want to focus as much as possible on these ads. To study among the 3-4 initially tested, which advertisement worked best, and then to start focusing more on what works well. Test new ads that are in the same style as the one that works best.

Your goal with ads is to come up with new ads that work better than the current ones. In conclusion, in the second stage, you want to study the results received and try to focus as much as possible on improving the AOV and advertising.

Moving on to the 3rd stage, here you should already be at a profit. You should not be able to enter stage 3 without being profitable.

Stage 3 is about scaling. You just can't climb if you're not profitable. Your goal is to make a profit first and then try to scale. Scaling can be done under many strategies. But the main idea is to focus more on what already works. It is important to understand that stages 1 and 2 are much harder, if you reach profitability and enter stage 3, scaling should not be so complicated. You have a much better perspective on promotion now.

Finish

I'm done with all 17 steps in which I have maximum confidence that will help you start dropshipping.

Decide to be a shark of entrepreneurship.

A shark who did not care about the surroundings, situations, and opinions of others.

A shark who is ready for action at any time.

A shark ready to act and do anything to achieve its goals.

A shark was hungry and extremely dangerous.

Become a shark of entrepreneurship!